History for Kids: Sumerian Mythology

www.dinobibi.com

Contents

Introduction

What humans call "civilization" didn't always exist. We didn't always live in big cities, have roads to get to places easier, or grow food on farms. For a long time, humans were hunter-gatherers. Hunter-gatherers wandered from place to place looking for food. They didn't build homes or stay in one place.

The Sumerians, as far as we know, were the first people to start a civilization. They built cities, raised animals, made pottery, and even had a government. Even though they lived a long time ago, we know a lot about them because they invented writing. The Sumerians carved words on stone tablets, and some of those tablets are still around today.

Sumerian writing on a wall

A few of these carvings are stories that tell us what the Sumerians believed in. They lived in a world where nature was everywhere, and they were at the mercy of it. Nature was a big part of their religion. They believed that nature was personified. When something is personified, that means it is given human characteristics and form when it normally wouldn't have them. For example, in the Sumerian religion, they personified the moon. We know the moon is a big space rock orbiting around the Earth. The Sumerians didn't know exactly what the moon was, so they thought a god walking around in human form controlled it. This god was the spirit of the moon. You'll learn all about the different Sumerian gods and goddesses in Chapter 3.

Some of the beliefs the Sumerians had might sound silly to us today. In the time the Sumerians lived, though, their stories made sense. Without the technology we have today, there was no other way to explain the world. These stories describing how the Sumerians thought the world worked are what we now call myths. Even though myths aren't true, they can tell us about what the world was like in ancient civilizations. Myths are the closest thing we have to time travel. Buckle up, because you're about to jump all the way back to 4000 BCE — 6,000 years ago.

Chapter 1:
Who were the Sumerians?

The Sumerian civilization, known as Sumer, started sometime between 4500 and 4000 BCE lasting almost 2,000 years, until 2004 BCE. That's a very long time! Compare that to the United States, which has only been a country for a little over 240 years.

The Sumerians did some pretty amazing things. They built huge cities and came up with canal systems to stop floods and water their crops. They also knew a little bit of science and could perform surgeries. They may have lived 6,000 years ago, but they were smart and knew how to take care of themselves.

Where Did They Live?

Sumer was located in Mesopotamia. Today, Mesopotamia doesn't exist anymore. The area that used to be Mesopotamia is now called the Middle East, where countries like Iraq and Syria are.

Syria and Mesopotamia retro map

Mesopotamia was part of the Fertile Crescent. The Fertile Crescent was an area of land where the world's first civilizations showed up. Sumer was one of those civilizations. The Sumerians lived in between two rivers, the Tigris and the Euphrates. People in ancient times usually lived near water because it was easier to survive there. Sometimes, though, if you lived too close to a river, your city could flood. But the Sumerians were smart.

Have you ever looked out the window when you're in a car and seen ditches on both sides of the road? Ditches are dips in the ground where water can flow, and they help keep roads safe when there's a lot of rain. The Sumerians used ditches to stop their cities from flooding when the rivers got too high.

8

They had to come up with ideas like ditches because they couldn't move their cities. Hunter-gatherers could move their campsites if flooding started, but the Sumerians were stuck in one place. There are a lot of good things about living in a city, but not being able to move around could be bad for civilizations that didn't invent things like ditches. What's the point of a city if it washes away?

Since the Sumerians were such good engineers and builders, parts of some of their cities are still around today.

What Was Life Like for Them?

While a lot of cultures in the past spent all day working in fields and struggled to survive, the Sumerians had it good. There were farms, of course, but there were also schools and temples. People could be farmers, teachers, business owners, fishermen, or many other things. That's why we call Sumer a civilization — there was more to do than just work in a field all day.

Rivers connected the cities in Sumer, so many cities had ships and docks where goods could arrive from somewhere else. Just like today, people paid for everything, so Sumerians were divided into four groups based on how much money they had and what jobs they could do. The priests were at the top, because it was their job to talk to the gods and figure out what they wanted. Next came the upper class and royalty. Life was good if you were in the upper class. The lower class came after the upper class, and at the bottom were the slaves.

Life wasn't easy even if you were a priest or royalty, though. The Sumerians thought that everything happened because one of their gods was either happy or mad. If the gods weren't happy, bad things would happen, and the Sumerians would do everything they could to make the gods happy again. If crops died, or it rained too much, or people got sick, it was all because they had made the gods mad. It must have been hard to try to figure out why someone you couldn't talk to was mad at your whole city!

What Did They Invent?

We can't talk about the Sumerians without mentioning some of their greatest inventions. Besides coming up with the first writing system (which you can read more about in the next section), the Sumerians invented some things that you might recognize.

The Wheel

Cars and bicycles certainly wouldn't be the same without the Sumerians. That's right, they were the first people to invent the wheel! The idea of a wheel is obvious to us today, but it wasn't obvious to people who had never heard of it. The Sumerians first used sledges, which have rails like Santa's sleigh that slide over the ground. Where the Sumerians lived, though, it didn't work very well. They had to come up with a better way of moving heavy things around, so that's why they came up with the wheel.

Chariots

Assyrian king on chariot hunting lion in Iraq

Another reason they needed the wheel was for the chariots they invented. Chariots are open carts pulled by one or two horses. The Sumerians used donkeys instead of horses, though. Chariots have two wheels, royalty used them to get around, and soldiers used them in battles.

Sailboat

Royal palace on a river with a sailboat

Since the Sumerians lived in between two rivers, they needed a good way to get around by water. The sailboats they invented were very simple, but they did the trick. They used lightweight wood for the main part and squares of fabric for the sails. Inventing the sailboat helped them get better at trading. The civilization that is better at trade is usually the one that lasts longer because it have more connections and money.

Math and Counting

Ancient Assyrian and Sumerian cuneiform from Mesopotamia

Yes, you can go ahead and blame the Sumerians if you want to. Although, you would probably still have to do math even if they hadn't come up with an early form of it. Since the Sumerians traded a lot and had such a big civilization, they needed a way to keep track of money and inventory. When it comes to money and things like bundles of wheat, sometimes you need to use big numbers. The Sumerians came up with symbols for big numbers. For example, a round ball shape meant 10, and a cone shape meant 60. Their counting system was based on the number 60 because it's a number you can count on your hands using five fingers on one hand and 12 knuckles on the other.

So, don't feel bad if you count using your fingers. The Sumerians did too!

Agriculture

Without an agricultural system, it's hard to have a civilization. Agriculture is organized farming. When a group of people learns how to plant crops and raise animals in a way that takes the least amount of effort and can feed a lot of people, they are practicing agriculture. The Sumerians were great at agriculture and even came up with irrigation, which is a way to water big fields filled with crops without having to go around with a can watering every plant.

What Language Did They Speak?

The language of Sumer was Sumerian. While most languages, like English, are related to other languages (like the Germanic languages for English), Sumerian is all by itself. People don't speak Sumerian anymore because it was replaced by another language called Akkadian.

Sumerian Writing

Sumerian was the first language written down, at least as far as we know, in a form called cuneiform. Sumerians invented cuneiform which was one of the very first writing systems. Sumerians were able to write books of poetry and keep track of things like money using cuneiform and clay tablets. Cuneiform uses symbols and something called "wedges." People made wedges by taking a reed stylus, which kind of looks like a chopstick, and pressing it into clay. When the clay hardened, it became a tablet. Some of these tablets still exist, and archeologists have figured out what some of the symbols mean.

Ancient clay letter

A lot of the cuneiform symbols are for combinations of letters, like 'b' and 'a' or 'a' and 'n,' which means there are many symbols. If you want to learn more about all the different symbols the Sumerians had, look up "cuneiform" on the Internet, and you'll find all sorts of pictures of real tablets!

What Happened to the Sumerians?

The Sumerians were around for 2,000 years, but why didn't they last longer? Around 2400 BCE, another civilization in the Fertile Crescent took over the Sumerians. The Elamites, who

15

lived in the area that is now Iran, broke into Ur, the main city of Sumer. While they were taking control of Ur, another group of people called Amorites were also taking over. Eventually, the Amorites also took control of the Elamites, so both the Elamites and the Sumerians became Amorites.

A lot of great ancient civilizations ended this way. Someone else with more weapons or money (or both) would take over, and the people of one culture would become people of a different culture.

Chapter 2:
The Sumerian Creation Story

The Sumerians had a very complicated creation story with four main gods who made everything, including the other gods. The gods came up with strict rules for how the universe should work, and everybody was supposed to follow those rules.

Before there was any universe, though, there was nothing except what the Sumerians called the "primeval sea." The sun, moon, planets, and everything else didn't exist until they were made in the primeval sea.

The Primeval Sea

A sea is just like an ocean, only smaller. No one knows how big the primeval sea in the creation myth was, but the goddess of water, Nammu, ruled the sea. She called the primeval sea "abzu," and inside abzu she gave birth to Heaven and Earth. The Sumerians called the primeval sea, Heaven, and Earth "an-ki," which means "Heaven-Earth." To them, an-ki was the universe.

When Nammu gave birth to an-ki, she also made the first four gods, An, Enlil, Enki, and Ninhursag. It was their job to take care of Heaven and Earth. First, they had to separate Heaven from Earth. Enlil was the one who did this, since he was the god of wind and air. In between Heaven and Earth, the gods made a barrier out of tin that went all the way around the Earth. Inside the tin barrier, Enlil made what the Sumerians called "lil," which means air. "Lil" became the atmosphere. Some spots inside the tin barrier had more lil than others. These spots became the sun, moon, and other planets.

After Enlil separated Heaven and Earth, each of the four gods decided which piece they wanted. An took Heaven, Enlil took the Earth and brought Ninhursag with him, and Enki took the Earth's water.

Creating Humans, Plants, and Animals

Making Heaven and Earth was great, but the gods knew it could get boring if it was just going to be the four of them in the universe. After Nammu made the universe, she told Enki to make humans with the help of Ninhursag.

Ninhursag used clay to make the first six people. Enki tried to make another person, but he did something wrong. The person Enki made couldn't eat or drink anything, and he couldn't talk. Enki and Ninhursag stopped making humans, so they wouldn't mess up again.

To keep the humans company, Enki, Enlil, and Ninhursag got together and made plants and animals. Now the Earth had everything it needed, and the gods could sit back and relax for a while.

The Nether World

Underground world illustration

The Sumerians believed a nether world was underneath the Earth. The nether world was where people went when they died. On Earth, they would bury the bodies, then their souls would float down to the nether world. There were special entrances to the nether world in Sumerian cities. No one left the nether world unless they could trade places with someone else still on Earth.

When a person's soul went to the nether world, it had to get on a boat and cross a river that would take them to a god named Utu. Utu was like a judge, and he would decide if the soul would get to be happy or unhappy in the nether world. If the person had been helpful and nice when he or she were alive, that person would be happy in the nether world. If he or she had been mean, the nether world would be a very sad and lonely place.

Two gods ruled the nether world together: Nergal and Ereshkigal. You'll learn more about both in the next chapter, along with all the other gods from the creation story.

Chapter 3:
Sumerian Gods, Goddesses, and Monsters

The Sumerians believed a god controlled everything, from the wind to the canals in their cities. Because of this, they had hundreds of gods and goddesses. Some historians even think there might have been a list of thousands at one point! Gods and goddesses are also called "deities," and the Sumerians worshipped a few main ones. They organized the deities based on how important they were. The four deities who took care of Heaven and Earth came first. These four were also part of a group of seven deities who "decreed the fates." You'll learn what that means soon. After these seven, there were fifty other deities called the Annuna, meaning An's children. Don't worry, you won't have to learn about every single deity!

Gods and goddesses each controlled a certain part of the world, but they could all walk around in human form. They did the same things humans do, like eat, drink, sleep, and fight. They could even get hurt and be killed. As long as they stayed safe, though, they were immortal. Immortal means they could live forever.

Nammu, The First Goddess

In the Sumerian creation story you just read about, Nammu was the very first goddess. She lived in the primordial sea that existed before everything else. In some ways, she was the primordial sea. She made Heaven and Earth along with the four main deities. It was also Nammu's idea to make humans.

Nothing else is known about Nammu. There are a lot of myths and stories that talk about what happened after she created the universe, but she isn't in any of them.

The Main Four Deities

The main four deities were also in the creation story. They were all made by Nammu after she gave birth to an-ki (Heaven-Earth). Each one played a special role in getting the world ready for humans.

An

In the beginning, An was the leader of the gods. He helped separate Heaven and Earth by taking Heaven for himself. To the Sumerians, he was the god of the heavens. Most of the fifty "great gods" that you'll learn about a little later are An's children.

People worshiped An in the Sumerian city of Uruk. There was a temple dedicated to him in the middle of the city.

Enlil

An was the leader of the gods when the universe was first made, but later Enlil took over. For most of their history, the Sumerians called Enlil the "king of all the gods" and "king of Heaven and Earth." He decided that Heaven and Earth should be separated. He also thought a tin barrier between Heaven and Earth was a good idea.

Enlil was the god of the air. He pulled Heaven and Earth apart by taking Earth while An took Heaven. Since Enlil had control of Earth in the beginning, he decided to make it look nice. He added plants (with the help of Enki and Ninhursag), then after humans were made, he invented plows and pickaxes. These were tools that humans used to plant and grow crops.

Early plow

When Enlil became the most powerful god, everyone had to listen to what he said. His word was law. Since the Sumerians saw him as the leader of the deities, they built a temple dedicated to him in Nippur, which was an ancient city in Mesopotamia. Nippur was the religious center of Sumer, which means that

23

most of the worshipping the Sumerians did happened there. It was kind of like a church, but the whole city was one big church. The temple for Enlil in Nippur was called the "Mountain House." It was the most important temple in all of Mesopotamia.

Enlil was the father of the moon god, Nanna. He was also the father of the nether world deities that you'll learn more about later in this chapter.

Enki

Enki was the god of the oceans on Earth, as well as wisdom. He controls something called the "Me," which lists the laws of the universe that every god follows.

Enki and Ninhursag made humans, and after that, Enki became the protector of humans. He was very important to the Sumerians because he oversaw taking care of the Earth. They believed that he helped make the land in Mesopotamia good for crops.

The Sumerians also believed that Enki knew magic and used it to rid the world of evil. Whenever someone got sick, they thought it was because there was a demon in that person. They would pray to Enki to get rid of the demon.

The Mesopotamian city of Eridu was where Sumerians worshipped Enki the most. They called his temple the "House of the Abzu," since he was the god of water and oceans.

Ruins of Eridu

Ninhursag

Ninhursag was known as the "mother of all beings." She had several names according to the Sumerians, including Ki, Ninmah, and Nintu. She was the goddess of pregnancy and childbirth. Together with Enki, she helped make humans. The Sumerians also called Ninhursag the Earth goddess because she helped Enlil and Enki make plants and animals so that the Earth would be full of life. They worshipped her in the city of Keš.

The Seven Deities Who Decreed the Fates

A decree is an official order from authority. For example, if your mom tells you to clean your room, you can think of that as a decree. The Sumerian seven gods who decreed the fates were the most important deities. These seven included the four main deities you just learned about, plus three others. All the deities that were part of the seven were very powerful.

Nanna

Nanna was the god of the moon. He shined with a light that came out of his body and rowed across the sky in a canoe-like boat called a gufa. He was the father of the other two deities in this list, Utu and Inanna.

Utu

Symbol of Utu

Utu was the god of justice and the sun. His father was Nanna and his mother was Ningal (you'll learn about her in the next section). If you remember from the last chapter, Utu was the judge who decided what happened to souls in the nether world. He stayed in the nether world during the night while Nanna was shining. In the morning, he came out and walked across the sky to let his light shine on the Earth.

Since Utu was out during the day and could see everything that happened, he became the god of truth. Sumerians used to pray to him when they wanted to know the truth about a person or situation.

Inanna

Statue of Inanna

Inanna was the most important goddess after Ninhursag. She was the goddess of love and war, the daughter of Nanna and Ningal, and Utu was her brother.

Inanna loved power. She once asked Enki to give her more powers, which he could do because he was the keeper of the Me (the rules of the universe). By giving her more Me, Enki gave her more control over the world.

Sumerian kings worshipped Inanna when they wanted more political power because she represented war in politics.

The Fifty "Great Gods"

After the seven deities who decreed the fates, there were fifty other gods and goddesses the Sumerians believed in. Not all of them are listed here, but the ones we know more about are.

The fifty "great gods" are sometimes called the Annuna, which means An's children. Some of the great gods aren't An's kids, though. Since there are so many gods and goddesses, we'll just tell you the most important things about some of them.

Ereshkigal – Queen of the nether world. Inanna's sister.

Nergal – Ruled the nether world with Ereshkigal.

Nergal

Ninlil – Mother of the moon god, Nanna. Wife of Enlil. She was a goddess of the wind and air.

Ningal – Nanna's wife, mother of Utu and Inanna.

Nanshe – Goddess of orphans and widows. She took care of people who were alone and needed help.

Nisaba – Goddess of writing. She helped Nanshe take care of orphans and widows.

Ninisinna – Goddess of the planet Venus. She was also called the morning star and the evening star.

Ninurta – God of the south wind. He was also a warrior.

Ashnan – Goddess of crops and grain. She helped farmers grow food.

Lahar – God of cattle. He took care of farm animals.

Emesh and Enten – Brothers who were both the gods of farmers. While Ashnan and Lahar took care of crops and animals on farms, Emesh and Enten took care of the people living on the farms.

Uttu – Goddess of clothes and plants.

Enbilulu – God of rivers. He took care of the two rivers that the Sumerians lived between, the Tigris and Euphrates.

Ishkur – God of storms. Enki put Ishkur in charge of wind, but he also controlled rain. If storms were severe, the Sumerians thought they might have made Ishkur mad.

Enkimdu – God of canals and ditches, which were important in Sumerian cities.

Kabta – God of pickaxes. A pickaxe was a tool the Sumerians needed for farming and planting crops. They even had a myth that told how the gods created pickaxes!

31

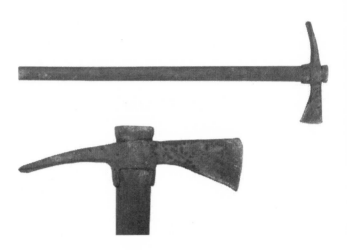

Pickaxe

Mushdamma – God of houses and fountains.

It might sound weird that the Sumerians had gods who oversaw things like houses and canals, but civilization was a new thing. It was important to them to protect what they had built, so they worshipped gods who could help keep the things they made safe.

Babylonian Deities

All the gods and goddesses we've talked about so far were part of the original Sumerian mythology. When the Babylonians took over the Sumerians, some part of their religion stayed the same, but a lot of names changed. There were even some new additions! In this section, we're going to take a quick look at some of the Babylonian gods and goddesses who were added to the list of Sumerian gods much later. Don't forget that the Sumerians didn't die out. They just became part of a different group of people, the Babylonians, and they kept a lot of their same beliefs.

Marduk

Sumerian Tablets and Marduk symbol

One of the most important gods the Babylonians added to Sumerian mythology was Marduk. He was the patron god of Babylon, which means he represented the Babylonians. Marduk was the king of the gods in the eyes of the Babylonians. He was the god of justice, healing, and magic. The Babylonians called him Bel, which means "Lord."

One of the main stories about Marduk tells of when he killed Tiamat, who was the Babylonian version of Nammu. In Babylonian stories, Tiamat wasn't a kind or motherly goddess like Nammu was to the Sumerians. Instead, Tiamat was a little bit crazy. When Marduk defeated her, the other gods recognized him as their leader, and he took over.

The Babylonians built a temple for Marduk and believed that he lived there. It was his job to take care of the people of the city, and it was the peoples' job to worship him.

Anšar and Kišar

When the Babylonians took over Sumer, they came up with their own creation story that was a little bit like the Sumerian one, but with a few different gods. One of those gods was Marduk, and two others were Anšar and Kišar (Kišar was a goddess). They are only in the Babylonian creation story and don't have any other role in Babylonian or Sumerian mythology.

They were some of the very first gods, along with Tiamat. Anšar and Kišar were husband and wife, and in the Babylonian story, An was their son. An's name in Babylonian myths was Anu.

Gula

Gula was the goddess of healing, and doctors worshipped her. She might have been a Sumerian goddess, too, but with a different name. Bau was the Sumerian goddess of dogs. In ancient times, people realized that wounds healed faster when a dog would lick them. Since gods can heal, and Gula is the goddess of healing, some people think that Gula might be the Babylonian version of Bau.

Girra

Girra might also have first been a god under a different name in Sumerian mythology. He was the god of fire and light. The Babylonians worshipped Girra because both fire and light are important for civilization. They also were a little bit afraid of him, though, because fire can burn and destroy if you're not careful.

Nabu

The Sumerians worshipped a lot of goddesses, and while men and women weren't equal in those days, women did have some freedom. Goddesses were important and were just as powerful as gods. When the Babylonians took over, though, they got rid of a lot of goddesses. They wanted to make the gods seem more powerful, so they replaced some of the Sumerian goddesses with gods. Nisaba was the goddess of writing to the Sumerians until the Babylonians replaced her with Nabu. The both did pretty much the same thing in both mythologies, though.

Sumerian and Babylonian Monsters

Every good story has to have monsters! Both the Sumerians and the Babylonians believed in monsters they called demons. While today we think of demons as evil spirits or bad creatures, not every demon in Sumerian mythology was evil. Demon just meant "spirit." Sometimes it's hard to tell if a demon started out in Sumerian mythology or Babylonian. The demons in this list could have come from either mythology, but we will try to let you know which one is more likely.

Pazuzu

Pazuzu is a very good example of a demon that was good. He was supposed to protect people from other demons – the ones that were evil. Whenever someone was afraid that Lamashtu, another demon, would get them, they asked Pazuzu for protection. Pazuzu had a human body, but his head looked like a monster and his feet had claws like an eagle.

Some people who study mythology think that Pazuzu was a Sumerian demon first, but he was more likely invented by the Babylonians.

Ugallu

Ugallu kept people safe from illness. He had a human body, bird's feet, and the head of a lion. He came from Babylonian mythology because he was one of the monsters Tiamat made in the Babylonian creation story. He was by himself in art and on pieces of jewelry, but later in Babylonian times, he started to be pictured along with a Sumerian demon, Lulal. Not a lot is known about Lulal other than that he was the goddess Inanna's son.

Scorpion People

Scorpion people were warriors who had scorpion tails, but the rest of their body was human. They pop up in the Babylonian creation story and Epic of Gilgamesh. They were supposed to protect against evil demons. In Epic of Gilgamesh, there were two scorpion people guarding a mountain that Gilgamesh wanted to climb. This mountain was where the sun would rise, so some people think that scorpion people worked for the sun god.

Mushhushshu

Detail of the ancient Babylonian Ischtar Tor

Mushhushshu means "furious snake." They were almost like dragons. Marduk, Enlil, and a few other gods rode on them to get around. Since both a Babylonian god and a Sumerian god had a pet mushhushshu, these monsters were probably part of both mythologies for a long time.

Lamashtu

Not all demons in mythology were evil, but Lamashtu was. Sumerians and Babylonians believed Lamashtu would take children, especially babies. Pregnant women would ask for Pazuzu to protect them and their babies from Lamashtu.

Besides being evil, Lamashtu was also scary looking. She had the head of a lioness, donkey teeth and ears, bird feet, and hair all over her body.

The Abgal

The Abgal were very important in Sumerian mythology. They were sages, which means they were very wise and were often the keepers of wisdom. The Abgal were Enki's seven sages. Enki was the keeper of the Me laws, but he used the Abgal to teach others about the Me. After the world was created, Enki sent the Abgal to Earth to teach the humans what the Me laws were and how to create civilization.

The humans would know that the Abgal were sages of the gods because they had the body of a fish and the head of a human. They also sometimes had wings.

Abgal were also in Babylonian mythology, but they were called the Apkallu. They either looked like fish people, humans with wings, or a griffin. A griffin is a mythological animal with the body of a lion and the head of an eagle.

Statue of a Griffin

Chapter 4:
Epic of Gilgamesh

Epic of Gilgamesh is a Sumerian epic poem. An epic poem is a long story about an amazing man or woman and the things he or she does. Epic of Gilgamesh is about King Gilgamesh.

The poem has survived for so long because it was written down on 12 clay tablets. Since it was written in cuneiform, we know most of what it says. The tablets were found in the ruins of a Sumerian library in the city of Nineveh. If you ever want to read Epic of Gilgamesh, all 12 stone tablets have been translated (written down in English or another language instead of cuneiform) and turned into a book!

As far as we can tell, Epic of Gilgamesh was probably written sometime between 2150 BCE and 1400 BCE. The real King Gilgamesh was alive around 1,000 years before the epic poem was written, so a lot of the stories, even the ones that don't have monsters in them, are probably made up.

Who Was Gilgamesh?

We know that there was a real King Gilgamesh because of letters and other official documents from Uruk that had his name on them. If we didn't have those, we might think he was a myth! That's how crazy some of the stories about Gilgamesh are.

The real Gilgamesh was the 5th king of Uruk. He ruled during the 26th century BCE, which was a period between 2600 BCE and 2501 BCE. When something happened so long ago, it's difficult to know exact dates.

All the stories about Gilgamesh make him sound like a hero. After he died, the people he ruled came up with such wild tales that he almost became like a god to them. If you know any stories about the legendary King Arthur, you have a pretty good idea of what Gilgamesh's people thought of him. Just like the beloved King Arthur is now more of a legend or myth than anything else, Gilgamesh is too.

A long time after Gilgamesh died, other kings pretended they were related to Gilgamesh so people would like them more. That tells you how big of an impact Gilgamesh must have had!

Epic of Gilgamesh is the only story we have about Gilgamesh. Some of it might be based on facts, but a lot of it is fantasy. No matter what the real king was like when he was alive, he sure did make an impact.

Summary of Epic of Gilgamesh

Epic of Gilgamesh starts out describing a vain, smug, and self-important king who thinks too much of himself. This person doesn't sound like the Gilgamesh that people would love, but according to the story, that's how he started out. In the poem, his mother is a goddess, and his father is both a priest and a king, making him part god and part priest. If you remember from the first chapter, priests and royalty were the most important people in Sumerian society.

The Sumerian gods were tired of Gilgamesh bragging and being annoying, so they decided it was time to take him down a notch. They sent a wild man named Enkidu, who was raised by animals and was a strong fighter. Enkidu challenged Gilgamesh to a fight. The gods thought Enkidu would win and if Gilgamesh lost, he might become a little humbler. Enkidu didn't win, though. Gilgamesh beat him, but instead of bragging about it and becoming even more smug, he and Enkidu became friends. They decided to set off into the world and have adventures together, which is what the rest of Epic of Gilgamesh is about.

Gilgamesh and Enkidu Fight Humbaba

The first battle in Epic of Gilgamesh is between the two friends and Humbaba, a monster who guarded the Cedar Forest. The Cedar Forest was where the gods lived. Everyone knew that a terrifying monster guarded the forest, but no one was brave enough to slay it. That is, until Gilgamesh showed up. Enkidu wasn't too happy about having to fight Humbaba, but Gilgamesh was his best friend, so he went along with the plan.

Together, the two of them were able to defeat Humbaba. Since the monster had been the guard of the home of the gods, the gods weren't happy Gilgamesh had killed it. Slaying Humbaba

43

wasn't the only thing the gods were mad at Gilgamesh for, though.

All the trees in the Cedar Forest were sacred. This means they were very special to the gods. No one was supposed to chop them down. In Epic of Gilgamesh, guess who didn't listen to the warning? That's right, Gilgamesh. He and Enkidu chopped down sacred trees to make a raft so they could get back home to Uruk. In the very first quest of Epic of Gilgamesh, the main character managed to anger all the gods.

Inanna and the Bull of Heaven

Defeating Humbaba was a big deal. While most of the gods were mad at Gilgamesh for doing it, one goddess was very impressed. Inanna, whom you might remember as the goddess of love and war, fell in love with Gilgamesh after he proved himself to be strong and courageous. Gilgamesh wasn't in love with Inanna, though. In mythology, rejecting a god or goddess is usually a bad idea. Inanna was so mad at Gilgamesh, she sent a monster known as the Bull of Heaven to kill him.

Gilgamesh and Enkidu had already beaten one monster, so they had no problem fighting the Bull of Heaven, too. They won the fight, which made Inanna even more mad. Since Enkidu was Gilgamesh's best friend, she killed Enkidu to get revenge.

Gilgamesh's Quest for the Meaning of Life

Enkidu's death made Gilgamesh realize he would die someday, too. He left Uruk and wandered around Mesopotamia, trying to figure out what the point of life was. Since he was half god and the gods were immortal, he couldn't accept that he would get old and die. He was part human, though, so a part of him knew that he would die if he didn't figure out a way to become immortal. Then, Gilgamesh remembered there was one human, Utnapishtim, who had become immortal.

Utnapishtim had survived something the Sumerians called the "Great Flood." The gods made him immortal since he had been brave and helpful during the Great Flood. The only problem was that Utnapishtim lived far away and was hard to find. Gilgamesh traveled over oceans, into forests, and across mountains while looking for Utnapishtim. Finally, after a long time wandering, he found the only person who might be able to help make him immortal.

Gilgamesh Fails to Become Immortal

Utnapishtim told Gilgamesh there were two ways to become immortal. These were really just tests to see if Gilgamesh was worthy of immortality.

In the first test, Gilgamesh had to stay awake for six days and seven nights. If you've ever stayed up past your bedtime, you know how hard it is not to fall asleep when you're tired! Since Gilgamesh had been walking for a long time looking for Utnapishtim, he couldn't stay awake for six days and seven nights. He didn't even last one day!

After failing the first test, Gilgamesh tried the second. For the second test, he was supposed to keep a magic plant safe. The moment he let his guard down, a snake ate the magic plant. Since he failed both tests, Utnapishtim didn't grant him immortality. Gilgamesh had to be okay with the fact that he would die someday.

Instead of being angry with Utnapishtim or trying to find another way to become immortal, Gilgamesh went home to Uruk. He decided to do his best to be a great king and have a happy life for however long he lived. Gilgamesh did die eventually, of course, but in a way, he did become immortal. Since Epic of Gilgamesh is a story that still exists, his name is still alive. We might have forgotten about most of the people who lived in the past, but we haven't forgotten Gilgamesh.

Why Epic of Gilgamesh is Important

Epic of Gilgamesh is a neat story, but is there any point to it? Someone took the time to write the entire poem on clay tablets, so it must mean something.

Besides being the first great work of literature, Epic of Gilgamesh tells us a lot about Mesopotamian culture. The themes in the book and the lessons Gilgamesh learned all tell us what was important to the Sumerians. They cared about having a good king, which is why Gilgamesh starts out as vain and selfish and in the end learns about being a good person (and a good king). The epic poem also tells us how the Sumerians viewed their gods. In the story, the gods punish Gilgamesh when he does things that make them mad. Every Sumerian, even the kings, could make the gods angry. No one was safe from them. Therefore, it was important in Sumerian culture to worship the gods and build temples dedicated to them. If you made the gods happy, your life was better.

The most important idea from Epic of Gilgamesh isn't what it can teach us about Sumerians, though. What most people take away from it is that even though life ends one day, that doesn't mean there's no point. Even though you won't be around forever, you should still do everything you can to be a good person. Life isn't pointless if you're not immortal like the gods. At least, the Sumerians didn't think so.

Chapter 5:
Stories from Sumerian Mythology

Epic of Gilgamesh isn't the only story from Sumerian mythology that's worth talking about. After the gods and goddesses put the universe together, they didn't just sit around. They went on adventures of their own, they invented things to help humans, and they generally had exciting lives. There are too many stories to put in one chapter, but we will talk about the important ones.

Sumerian Flood Myth

Just like in Christianity, the Sumerians had a flood myth. Both flood stories might be based on a real flood that happened thousands of years ago. Since the Sumerians didn't know exactly what causes a flood like we do, they thought they had angered a god who was punishing them. They came up with an entire story about why a god was mad, why he sent a flood, and how humans survived.

The Sumerian Flood Myth was written on a clay tablet, but the tablet broke and now all we have is the bottom part. That means we don't know the whole story, but we know enough of it to guess what the rest says.

The story probably started out by explaining how humans were created. You already know some of this story from an earlier chapter. Basically, Ninhursag and Enki took some clay and formed it into humans. Then, for some reason, Enlil decided that he wanted to wipe out humanity. We don't know why because the part of the story explaining Enlil's reasoning is missing. It could have been because humans made him mad, he didn't like how loud they were, or he was bored that day. No one knows for sure.

Enki heard that Enlil was going to destroy every human by starting a flood. Since Enki had helped create humans, he didn't want anything bad to happen to them. He decided to warn someone to build a boat. In Epic of Gilgamesh, the name of the king was Utnapishtim. However, he goes by a different name, Ziusudra, on the tablet with the flood myth written on it. Since the original story uses Ziusudra as the name of the boat builder, we will too.

Ziusudra listened to Enki's advice and built an ark, which is a big boat. We don't know exactly how he built the ark or what it looked like because the part of the tablet describing this part is gone. We do know that he was able to build the ark, though.

Noah's Ark

The flood came, and it lasted for seven days and nights. All the people Ziusudra allowed on the ark survived, so Enlil was not able to wipe out humanity. He wasn't very happy with this, but Enki was somehow able to convince him not to hurt any more humans.

Since Ziusudra had listened to the advice of one of the gods and saved people, he was granted immortality. The next time he pops up is in Epic of Gilgamesh.

Healing Enki's Wounds

Some of the gods and goddesses we haven't talked about yet were born in the story about Enki and how Ninhursag healed his wounds. Before we can talk about them, though, you need to know how Enki got hurt in the first place.

Uttu, you might remember, was the goddess of plants. In this story, she created eight beautiful plants. Before she could take care of them and make more, though, Enki came along and ate every single one. Uttu was so upset, she went to Ninhursag for help. To punish him, Ninhursag cursed Enki. Gods and goddesses usually can't die, but they can get hurt. Ninhursag's curse put eight wounds on Enki since he had eaten eight plants. These wounds started to drain Enki's life. After cursing him, Ninhursag disappeared.

By this time, Enki was sorry he had eaten the plants. He asked Enlil for help, but Enlil didn't know where to find Ninhursag. He asked a fox to track her down, so the fox did. When Ninhursag came back, she wasn't angry anymore. She even felt a little sorry for Enki. She decided that he had been punished enough, so she removed the curse.

It wasn't easy to do, though. The only way to remove the curse was to turn the eight wounds into something else. Since Ninhursag is known as the mother goddess, she was able to turn the wounds into new gods and goddesses. These deities were:

- Abu – King of plants
- Nintul – Lord of Magan (a region of Sumer)
- Ninsutu – Married Ninazu, who was an underworld god
- Ninkasi – Goddess of the heart and healing
- Nazi – Married the goddess of wisdom, Nanshe

- Dazimua – Married Ningishzida, who was one of the underworld gods
- Ninti – Goddess of life
- Enshagag – Lord of Dilmun (a region of Sumer)

Once all the new gods and goddesses had been made, Enki was healthy again.

Creation of the Pickaxe

As strange as it sounds, the Sumerians had an entire myth about how the pickaxe was created. This tool helped them grow crops and build things, so it was an important part of their culture.

In the pickaxe story, Enlil creates it. When he made the pickaxe, he also invented the idea of "labor," which is hard work that is usually physical, like working in a field. The story also says that Enlil made the pickaxe "exalted," which means it is very important.

The first pickaxe that Enlil made was gold with lapis lazuli, which is a type of blue gemstone. He gave it to humans as a gift; then, the other gods gave the pickaxe powers. We don't know exactly what those powers are, though.

Lapis lazuli

At the end of the pickaxe creation story, there is a list of everything the pickaxe can do. According to the story, a pickaxe can help build cities and houses, make people respect their king, crush bad plants, tear up roots, and help good plants grow.

This short but simple story shows us how important tools were in the Sumerian culture. It also tells us that the Sumerians believed their gods were responsible for everything, even inventions.

Inanna in the Underworld

There are so many stories about Inanna. The Sumerians were fascinated by her, and the many tales they came up with prove that. One of her most well-known stories is about her "descent into the underworld." The underworld is the same as the nether world that we talked about in an earlier chapter. We mentioned this story in Chapter 3, but it deserves to be explained a little more.

The Descent of Inanna is a poem written in cuneiform on a clay tablet sometime between 3500 and 1900 BCE. The story starts out with Inanna deciding she has enough power in Heaven, but she doesn't have any in the underworld. If you remember from Chapter 3, Ereshkigal, the Queen of the underworld, is Inanna's sister. Inanna thought that she might be able to get more power from her sister. At least, if she asked nicely.

No one could just go into the underworld whenever he or she wanted, though. Not even goddesses. Inanna had to wait for a reason to go. After Gilgamesh and Enkidu killed the Bull of Heaven, there was a funeral in the underworld because the bull was Ereshkigal's husband. This made him Inanna's brother-in-law.

When Inanna tried to get into the underworld for the funeral, Ereshkigal found out about it and locked her out. Seven gates led to the underworld, and Ereshkigal would only let Inanna through them if she would hand over a piece of her clothing at each gate. Inanna's clothes gave her power, so by the time she got through the seventh gate, all her powers were gone. After the seventh gate, she went to the throne room where her sister was, and Ereshkigal turned her into a corpse. Talk about sibling rivalry!

Luckily, before she left for the underworld, Inanna had told one of her servants to go to one of the gods for help if she didn't come home after the funeral. When Inanna didn't come home, the servant went to Enki for help. Enki sent two of his own servants to bring her back. They were able to wake her up, but Ereshkigal wouldn't let them leave without a trade.

Almost everyone outside of the underworld was very sad, because they thought Inanna had died. The only person who didn't seem sad was Inanna's husband, Dumuzi. Inanna was angry that he didn't seem to miss her, so she decided that he should be the one to take her place in the underworld. Dumuzi didn't want to go, so his sister offered to go instead. Ereshkigal made them a deal so everyone would be happy. Inanna could leave the underworld, but only if Dumuzi would stay there for half the year and his sister, Geshtinanna, would stay there for the other half.

This very long story tells us how the Sumerians explained the way the seasons change. Whenever Dumuzi was in the nether world, Geshtinanna controlled autumn and winter, and when Dumuzi was out of the nether world, it was spring and summer.

A lot of other mythologies have a story like this. The Greeks, for example, also have a story about a goddess being trapped in the underworld for part of the year.

The Sacred Me

We've mentioned the Me once or twice, so it's about time we tell you what it is. This isn't a story, exactly, but some of the myths discuss the Mes.

First, what's a Me? A Me is almost like an order from the gods. It describes how something in the world is supposed to work and tells both the gods and humans what they need to do. Every Me is a rule that no one can break. Some of the Mes are physical objects, and some are words or ideas. The collection of all the Mes, kept by Enki, is called the Sacred Me.

Two main stories, Enki and the World Order and Inanna and Enki – The Transfer of the Arts of Civilization, talk about the Mes and describe what they are.

Enki and the World Order

The first story with the Sacred Me, Enki and the World Order, talks about what Enki did with the all the Mes after he got them from Enlil. In the story, Enki went to each city in Sumer and gave out some of the Mes. The Mes would help each city thrive, but every city received a different Me and a different purpose. One city received "success in war," while another got "abundant crops." While he was handing out the Mes, he also helped all the gods and goddesses figure out what they were supposed to do. In every city, he decided which god and goddess would be the best fit.

Inanna and Enki – The Transfer of the Arts of Civilization

While everyone else had a special job that was just for them, Inanna felt like she didn't have anything to do. She complained to Enki and asked if she could have some of the Mes. She thought that if she had some Mes, she would have more power. He wasn't going to give her any, but she was so sad that he finally gave in.

What Enki didn't know is that Inanna secretly wanted to make the city that worshipped her more wealthy and powerful. Her city was Erech, and she thought that if she could make it a popular city, more people would worship her.

The Mes that Enki gave to Inanna included: lordship, godship, priestly offices, truth, music, heroship, leather worker, metal worker, and so much more. All these Mes would help make a city strong, popular, and wealthy.

As soon as Inanna had all the Mes she wanted, she put them on a boat and sailed to Erech. While she was on her way, Enki realized that he had done something bad and tried to stop her. He sent sea monsters into the river to get to her before she could reach Erech, but she made it there anyway. Inanna gave the Mes to the city, and everyone (except Enki) was happy. The rest of the story is gone, so no one knows if Inanna's plan worked and she became more popular when the city became richer, or if nothing changed.

The List of Mes

Both stories mention over 100 Mes, which is too many to put in this book! We'll just mention a few of them and explain what they mean. Remember that Mes can be words, ideas, or physical objects. The Sumerians never wrote about which Mes were just ideas and which were things that you could hold and use, but we can guess on some of them.

The exalted and enduring crown – A long time ago, kings ruled for their entire lives, then when they died, another member of their family took over. The exalted and enduring crown means that a king can rule for as long as he lives, and everyone has to respect him and look up to him. Remember the Sumerians made up the Mes as part of their mythology. This Me was a very important one to have because it was a way of explaining why kings were allowed to have power over everyone else. If the gods declared it, no one could argue.

The throne of kingship – This Me was another that explained why kings were allowed to be kings. If they claimed that the gods gave them the "throne of kingship" Me, that was the law and nobody could say differently.

The royal insignia – This symbol is one of a family or group. For example, insignias are military patches that tell you what rank someone is. Kings and queens had royal insignias they would wear and put on things they owned so people would recognize them and know what belonged to them.

Art – The Me of art gave a city or a person the ability to draw, paint, or sculpt beautiful artwork. The Sumerians thought that artistic ability was a skill or gift given by the gods.

Music – Just like art, music was a Me only special people received. If you didn't have the Me of music, no one would listen or think your music was good.

The destruction of cities – Most of the Mes seemed like good things, but there were a few bad ones too. Just like there are bad things in the world, there are also bad things in the Sacred Me. The destruction of cities gave a god, another city, or one person the ability to wipe out another city. Enki wanted to protect the Sacred Me because some of the Mes were like this one. In the wrong hands, bad things could happen.

Wisdom – To the Sumerians, smart people weren't just smart on their own. Intelligence, or wisdom, was a gift from the gods. Wisdom isn't just knowing things, though. It means knowing what to do with the knowledge you have.

Fear – This Me is another of the less positive ones. The Sumerians believed every emotion was a Me that could be given or taken away. Fear was one of these emotions.

Chapter 6:
Sumerian Mythology in Today's World

The Sumerians lived a long time ago, so why do we still care about the myths they believed in? For starters, they were the world's first civilization. They also created the first writing system and wrote the first epic poem. The Sumerians represent a huge step in the history of humans. Any culture or society that is the first to do something is worth studying.

Besides inventing books, which we couldn't imagine living without today, the Sumerians also came up with time. Well, sort of. Time already existed, of course. The Earth moves around the Sun and spins on its axis. The day starts when the sun is up and ends when the sun goes down. That's a pretty simple way to look at time, and for most of human history, that's what people did. The Sumerians weren't happy with this way of understanding time, though. They divided up the day into minutes and hours, just like we do today. In fact, if the Sumerians hadn't decided that there are sixty seconds in a minute, and sixty minutes in an hour, our clocks today might look very different!

Since so many things we still have today came from the Sumerians, it makes sense to look closely at their mythology to see if there's anything else they can teach us.

Sumerian Mythology and Other Religions

We didn't just get books and timekeeping from the Sumerians. Their beliefs and stories from their mythology inspired a lot of other religions, too. A lot of the famous stories in the Bible came from Sumerian myths.

In the last chapter, you read about the Sumerian flood myth. Did you notice how similar it is to the story of Noah's ark from the Bible? In both tales, a god is mad at humans and sends a flood to kill everyone. The god warns one person, and he builds an ark to save people. Since the Sumerian flood myth came first, and the Sumerians wrote everything down, the person who wrote about Noah's ark probably used the Sumerian story as inspiration.

The Garden of Eden is another story from the Bible that is a lot like a Sumerian story. In Epic of Gilgamesh, Enkidu lived in a beautiful forest with animals until the gods needed him to fight Gilgamesh. To get Enkidu out of the forest, they sent a woman in with food. Enkidu wasn't allowed to eat anything that wasn't from the forest or he would be kicked out. He ate the food anyway and had to leave. The same thing happened to Adam and Eve in the Garden of Eden story.

Conclusion

Whew, what a wild ride! There certainly was a lot to learn about the Sumerians, and there's still a lot this book didn't cover. Isn't it amazing how we know so much about people who lived millennia before us?

The biggest gift the Sumerians gave to us is literature. Without books, the world would be emptier and a lot sadder, too. Even though we have the Internet, there is so much you can learn from books. Almost everything we know about the Sumerians we learned from the tablets they left behind. So, when you're reading about them, just remember that you have an ancient scribe (someone who sat down with a big chopstick and a lump of clay to draw symbols in) to thank.

Or, if you believe the Sumerians, you can thank the goddess of writing, Nisaba!

More from us

Visit our book store at: www.dinobibi.com

History series

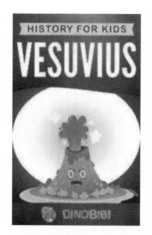

Travel series

Made in the USA
Middletown, DE
08 September 2022

73501275R00040